VOLUME 104 OF THE YALE SERIES OF YOUNGER POETS

JUVENILIA

Ken Chen

Foreword by Louise Glück

Yale UNIVERSITY PRESS

New Haven and London

Designed by Nancy Ovedovitz and set in Scala type by Keystone Typesetting, Inc. Printed in the United States of America.

Library of Congress Cataloging-in-Publication Data
Chen, Ken, 1979–
Juvenilia / Ken Chen ; foreword by Louise Glück.
    p.   cm. — (Yale series of younger poets ; 104)
ISBN 978-0-300-16007-9 (alk. paper) — ISBN 978-0-300-16008-6 (pbk. : alk. paper)
I. Title.
PS3603.H449J88 2010
811'.6—dc22
2009052146

A catalogue record for this book is available from the British Library.

This paper meets the requirements of ANSI/NISO Z39.48-1992 (Permanence of Paper).

10 9 8 7 6 5 4 3 2 1

CONTENTS

Poetry students in the 1960s were fond of a game based on renga, the Japanese collaborative form that alternates stanzas of seventeen and fourteen syllables. The classical form depends on the principles of link and shift, what Basho called "refraining from stepping back," each individual stanza both connected to and evolving from its predecessor. In Stanley Kunitz's twentieth-century classroom, the poem rotated clockwise from student to student; for "poem" read a piece of paper folded backward from the top, so that each of us saw only that stanza directly preceding the one we were about to write, which we hoped would be both boldly formal and mathematically perfect. The whole, to which the increasing thickness of the fold alluded, was unknowable: its progressive temporary vanishing facilitated our Basho-like refraining: there was no world to step back into. Narrative, trajectory, sustained meditation around a single set of ideas, these conventions by which we practiced a form, were precluded by the renga's methodical opacity; it restricted from view nearly everything that came before. Instead we made a chain of associations, each moment connected only to the two adjacent, making the last stanza often entirely remote from the first.

Retrospectively, a poem of this kind acquired a distinct psychological aura: it suggested a mode of being characterized by disconnection, requiring a compensatory intensity of focus on immediate detail. In place of a single governing idea or story, we relied on inference and improvisation: the past was buried or denied (folded over) though it continued imperiously to shape the present. Coexisting with heightened sensitivity to the moment was a constant intuition of something vast or crucial, veiled, but still limiting or directing choices. One analogue to this state might be the immigrant experience, what Ken Chen calls "the Peking opera of my childhood."

Strange passengers in a stationary Acura, in what might be a parking lot, might also be a film lot: a father who drops the keys in the toilet, a mother "like the moon which rents light from the past," a small boy, an ancient Chinese poet (long dead), and, floating through the scene like a bit player in a crowd scene who goes where needed, an equally remote dreamlike grandfather who seems a character in a surreal gangster movie:

> The suitcase open on the bed.
> My grandfather is packing up his organs.
> When he is done, he takes a taxi to my grandmother's house for
>   supper.
> Exits the empty car to Taipei alley.

Dissolve. Now the Los Altos lot.

So did you listen to him, my Father says, taking his keys out of the
ignition. You should become a lawyer but your grandfather says
anything is fine. As long as you're the best.

My Father stays, my Mother stays silent. I sit and suck my
thumb.

I saw your painting. It was beautiful, my Mother says to
Wang Wei, restrained beside me by backseat-belt and streetlight world.
. . .

California moon not glow—or as the translation might say,
    irradiates instead . . .

and later:

                                You're young, my Father says,
I'm not sure to me or Wang Wei . . .
    and then Wang Wei:

        Red hearts in the southern country.
        Spring comes with stems enlarging.
        I didn't know you two were still together.

We're not, my Father says. . . .
                        My Father and Mother Decide My Future and
                        How Could We Forget Wang Wei?

The dead poet, dutifully dragged into the twentieth century, is no
more adrift than the other hostages, including the nascent poet, rep-
resentative of the first generation's amnesia. In their experience, the
present does not build on the past; it replaces the past. Normal evolu-

tionary modifications yield to something more radical and violent, the early self less changed than buried, its memories incapable of mutation or incorporation. Memories of this kind, of a lost world, are frozen: they exist independent of the present, in no relation to it. On the surface, the present may seem to outsiders enviably free, the past not close enough to reproach it or dictate to it. In fact, the present is haunted or crippled precisely because it cannot contain the past in a way that might change one's perception of it.

In this world, cryptic non-sequitur and silence often substitute for disclosure. The alternative: the child/poet comes to his vocation for speech unwittingly, body-first, via his "garrulous rash that tells my skin all the secrets of my body." He has, by now, instead of one car, two households; instead of a dead poet, a sibling:

> He asked about his parents, why they split up in the first place, what were they like when they were his age? My father—my mom's roommate from thirty years ago reveals—would mill around my mother's place every day, inspect the grass . . .
>
> There are two types of trees in winter,

But in general, "They don't talk about these things, my parents, who are as talkative as trees." What does talk is the world outside the family: doctors and waiters are mines of information, not all of it useful:

> At the doctor's office I watch the doctor's wall. A new flu bulletin! Have good posture!

or

> The waiter at Jade Pavilion thinks my mother is my sister. The waiter walks up and says, "It doesn't matter that no one is home, we still love her." He pours the tea and asks, "What good is eternal youth if no one loves you?"

later

> She takes me to the last doctor. Doctor number seven. Who jerks his finger in the air and says "Ah Penicillin! Penicillin muddies the waters!" and his hair plugs rustle like a lawn in suburbia.

Juvenilia is not, however, in its primary impulses autobiographical. Ken Chen is far too sophisticated and ambitious a poet to have written a local or sentimental book. The power and originality of this collection owe in part to Chen's use of immigrant displacement as a metaphor for the adult's relation to his childhood, or origins. No accident that the child is trapped in the backseat with the dead poet: over and over in these poems, the lost homeland corresponds to the vanished world of childhood and the adult speaker to the immigrant. The first world is gone: no one who knew it will talk about it. What survives is a vivid (sometimes paralyzing) conviction that, like the folded over stanzas, it determines the present.

"The Invisible Memoir" is a tour de force on these themes; the defining thread of abandonment holds together diverse forms:

My gold sword sunk into the ground.
My spirit lost among the long weeds.
Then in the cool night. Then in the quiet sky. Then the moon
    blossoming open.
My mind goes back to those old hallways, but now only
the light glows hollow on the waters of Ch'in-huai.

Uncle's house—the happiest time of my life.

Staying—fate
3rd daughter
Grandfather—divorce
Your son is having an affair.
The same price
I pay for the son, you pay for the daughter.

So the poem proceeds, a collage of exquisite, elusive translations, strange lists and outlines in which an entire human drama is contained, conversations, opinions, homilies, verdicts, scenes:

I sit with my sister on my grandmother's couch, where we stare at the coffee table and chew dried sour plums and wafers of Chinese candy, like a pink roll of pennies. My mother would measure our height against our grandmother, who with her husband had fled Beijing for Taipei. . . . When my mother was homesick, she thought of Taiwan, unlike her mother who thought of China. My grandmother had acquired a patience that wanted nothing—a sort of contented despair. . . .

"The Invisible Memoir" tells one person's story implicitly; explicitly it is if not exactly dynastic, a portrait of a culture. The deliberate blurring and overlapping of narrative voices point to thematic recurrences and repetitions. Here, as throughout the book, the first-person pronoun is markedly mobile, only occasionally attached to the artist or his persona. Chen's method is unique: a sort of narrative through excision (the formal correlative of discretion) like a diary with pages torn out, or an account of a complicated past thought to be suitable for a child's ears, the disturbing material prominently deleted. The fragments that exist have to count for a great deal, for everything. Hence the coaching, sometimes by the poet, sometimes by one of the other figures (though it is not always clear who speaks): "Fate is a trap," we are reminded, "but context is dynamic." And a general textbook for living: "Don't gossip / Live in the past." Beyond virtuosity, there is in this (as in many of Chen's poems) a resonant, pervasive echoing, the sense of an earlier language underlying the English lines, faintly distorting them or shifting emphasis. (A striking example of this occurs in "Taipei Novel," one section of which ends with a strangely unforgettable line: "When I am alone, I feel penitent, my heart damp like cold metal." It took me several readings to register the fact that the line is a perfect seventeen syllables, a linear haiku. In other words, the embedded past.)

The blurred identities and boundary confusions of "The Invisible Memoir" take other forms in this book, sometimes direct, comic, and sometimes, as in the love poems, sustained, so that love becomes a kind of quicksand, dissolving individuality. There seems sometimes only the haziest boundary between self and other, self and world:

She said to her husband, "Last night
my life was so quiet that my feelings were audible.
When the phone rang, I thought it was my heart."

Taipei Novel

Elsewhere, this blurring produces a false reasoning, cause and effect
hopelessly intertwined:

And the waters swallow him—are like the tears you shed.

Then he must not be swimming, for there were no tears . . .

The protagonist, like the reader, must play detective, sniffing out essential facts. Ordering them is another issue.

If it does not simply create panic, the absence of apparent causal relations, together with the scale and frequency of change, stimulates analytic capacities: what experience and memory cannot supply, intelligence infers or pieces together. Pattern and cause can be hypothesized. Chen is obsessed, though, with the defects of this process: logic, which is synthetic, cannot substitute for knowledge; the passion invested in logic mirrors the voids and gaps of memory—the more crucial the gaps, the more passionate the stake in logic.

Ken Chen is a lawyer by education, but these tendencies do not simply reflect training in law. Rather, the habits of mind and disposition that make an effective lawyer (and predispose someone to seek this training) make, in an artist, art of this kind: on the surface, cool, fastidious, obsessive; underneath, daring, relentless. Reasoning is taken to a level of scrupulousness that seems a new form of surrealism:

> Love is like tautology in the same way *like* is like tautology. Both are technologies with which we can turn one thing into another. *Like* for example turns an object around until we realize that what we had thought was a moon had actually been something else entirely—a pearl perhaps. . . . Love too is about turns. It begins with turning my head to meet your eye and ends when I turn away from you, lost. . . . The middle of love—when we forget that love is what describes us—occurs when I turn to you for everything: to learn how to sleep, to remind myself that yes I too possess a body and slowly it seems life conveys forward only so I have something to tell you at dinner. Time passes and I know you so well that these two terms—I and You (henceforth, "U")—grow indivisible, are the same. . . . Friendship is an expression; love is an equation.

> Yet even equations can be unhappy . . .
> "Love is like tautology in the same way *like* is like tautology"

The poem goes on to enact a series of crises and failures of feeling, abstract but recognizable, the symbols increasingly baroque, increasingly poignant. The end returns to the simplicities of the beginning:

> I call you up to tell you this, but no one answers the phone. Should I go home to see you? I do. There is no U. I is only me, me without you. There is a word for this. When there is only I, when I equals I—we call this an identity.

The confusion love creates with its overeagerness to replace the orphan self with a composite self is partly a confusion of conflicting extreme responses. Love creates feelings both ecstatic and terrifying—a composite self, a "U" or union, mends the wounds of childhood; it also contributes to its obsolescence; the past vanishes in being healed.

Bravura poems work here because there is, at the book's heart, such deep sadness, such wistfulness, such piercing awareness of ir-reconcilable, immutable needs. Likewise the aphorisms, which in other hands might seem trivial, an exercise in willed charm: these blossom, late in the collection, into a string of pithy, preemptive one-liners that both initiate and end conversations. Sometimes one hears the tone in which a parent silences a child:

> Longing would be so much easier without the other person obstructing it.
> The City of Habits

and:

> Just because you are the victim does not mean that you are not the perpetrator.

and:

> Why do we cover our mouths in embarrassment? Once we have seen the fangs we can never forget them.

Some of these moments are ascribed to Confucius, the father of all pith:

How I have gone downhill! It has been such a long time since I have
dreamt of the Duke of Chou.

Taipei Novel

And in the end, the great man by the river:

What passes away is, perhaps, like this. Day and night it never lets up.

These moments occur in a long anecdotal account of an affair,
doomed, filled with imbalances, the lovers meeting in the one place,
at the one time in which they can come together. The dreamlike re-
sult makes a poem in which each moment seems to be memorialized
as it occurs.

Great sophistication and high style often flourish at the expense of
emotional range. It may be more accurate to say that they are strat-
egies to mask a deficit. The miracle of this book is the degree to which
Ken Chen manages to be exhilaratingly modern (anti-catharsis, anti-
epiphany) while at the same time never losing his attachment to
voice, and the implicit claims of voice: these are poems of intense
feeling; they have isolated and dramatized the profound dilemma of
the adult's relation to childhood in poems of riveting intelligence and
sharp wit and austere beauty.

Reading for a competition such as this involves reading very few
books that are not well made. But current systems of education and
standards of judgment have tended to produce bodies of work in
which a kind of airbrushed polish obscures eccentricity and real dis-

tinction. Imagine, among a hundred-odd collections, many of them impressive, coming on a book called *Juvenilia*, with its delicious knowingness and sly collusive irony: the title alone staked a flag at the edge. If this is juvenilia, it seems to say, the earth is flat. Or, alternatively: this is juvenilia in that I, the poet, am young; then imagine the work of my maturity—

Here clearly was a poet who felt it was not enough for him to be good or even brilliant in one of the period manners—here was someone who meant to be individual, electric. The scale of the gift is more than equal to the dare. Like only the best poets, Ken Chen makes with his voice a new category:

> Your son? asks Wang Wei. He has seen me and become real, as
> though a ghost could die into a man. Not the monk you quite expect,
> Wang Wei wears a cowboy's deadened face and stares
> at you not unlike an establishing
> shot. . . .
>
> And Wang Wei asks Who are you?
> And my Father says Decide.
> > My Father and My Mother Decide My Future and
> > How Could We Forget Wang Wei?

Louise Glück

ACKNOWLEDGMENTS

To my family.

This book would not have been possible without the generosity of Louise Glück. Working on this manuscript with her has been a true delight and a life-changing mentorship and friendship.

Special thanks to the following people who have provided extensive comments on the poems in this manuscript: Megan Pugh, Catherine Barnett, Huan-Hua Chye, Will Clark, Miranda Field, Jennifer Hayashida, Beth Hillman, Sarah Karmazin, Katy Lederer, Phu Nguyen, Andrew Pogany, Brenda Shaughnessy, Maxwell Yim, and my poetry professors at the University of California at Berkeley, Stephen Booth, Anne Carson, Anne Cheng, Robert Hass, Robert Polito, and Ishmael Reed. Additional thanks to The Asian American Writers' Workshop.

Additional acknowledgment and thanks to the editors of the following journals who published versions of the work contained herein:

Echo, *The Berkeley Poetry Review*

My Father and My Mother Decide My Future and How Could We Forget Wang Wei?, *Palimpsest*

Taipei Novel, *The Kyoto Journal*

Anti-Tantalus, *Barrow Street*

The City of Habits, *Fence*

It Is a City You See Through Water, *Jubilat*

Additionally, the translations of Wang Wei and Li Yu contained within "My Father and My Mother Decide My Future and How Could We Forget Wang Wei?" and "The Invisible Memoir" were published in 5 *Fingers Review, The Boston Review of Books, The Yale Journal of Translation,* and *Fascicle.* Sections of "Taipei Novel" previously appeared in *Field, The Kyoto Journal,* and *Palimpsest.*

The italicized text in "Echo" is excerpted from the songs "Cross Road Blues (Crossroads)" and "Hell Hound on My Trail" by Robert Johnson. The line "Out it tumbles, hot, scalding, mixed, marvelous, terrible, oppressive!" from "Taipei Novel" is from an essay by Virginia Woolf titled "The Russian Point of View"; the dialogue from Confucius in the same poem is adapted from D. C. Lau's translation of *The Analects.* The last section of the book, "The Invisible Memoir," relies on a variety of materials, which are listed on page 77—most notably, Daniel Bryant's *Lyric Poets of the Southern Tang* and *Strange Stories from a Chinese Studio* written by Pu Song-Ling and translated and annotated by Herbert Giles. Giles's footnotes serve as the origin of a quotation that is cited in text, as well as the following text not attributed within the poem: "The tears of Chinese mermaids are said to be pearls"; "The great sorrow of decapitation as opposed to strangulation is that the body will appear in the realms below without a head. The family of any condemned man who may have sufficient means will always bribe the executioner to sew it on again"; and "Which, well cooked, are a very good substitute for asparagus." The poems in this collection also quote from the following works, which are cited in text: *The Art of Chinese Poetry* by James Liu, *Law and Revolution: The Formation of the Western Legal Tradition* by Harold Berman, and *The Journal of Jules Renard,* edited and translated by Louise Bogan and Elizabeth Roget.

1.

MY FATHER AND MY MOTHER DECIDE MY FUTURE AND HOW COULD WE FORGET WANG WEI?

The suitcase open on the bed.
My grandfather is packing up his organs.
When he is done, he takes a taxi to my grandmother's house for
   supper.
Exits the empty car to Taipei alley.

Dissolve. Now the Los Altos lot.

So did you listen to him, my Father says taking his keys out of the
ignition. You should become a lawyer but your grandfather says
anything is fine. As long as you're the best.

My Father stays, my Mother stays silent. I sit and suck my
thumb.

I saw your painting. It was beautiful, my Mother says to
Wang Wei, restrained beside me by backseat-belt and streetlight
world—Wang Wei who says:

In the silent bamboo woods, sitting along
Playing strings and bellowing long.

But America is allergic to bamboo, my Father says to Wang Wei. They
love skill sets, cash and the first person singular,
the language of C++ not our English. Steps out,
shuts the door, puts gas pump by Acura trunk. My father's son
does not understand, forgets the Chinese
he never remembered. But my mother holds words in her mouth:
    The Peking opera soundtrack of my childhood.
You sound like it. I'd listen to it on the radio. You know, when I had to
sweep the floor. And then Wang Wei:

    Nobody knows but the deep grove
    and the luminous moon that glows in response.

California moon not glow—or as the translation might say, irradiates
    instead
like beige screen before my Mother, now at HP after Taipei and
    degree in Home Ec
and divorce. My Mother like the moon which rents light from its past,
my Mother who says, looking at the dashboard, You should listen to
your father. I don't know. Here he comes.
    My Father unlocks the door and says, Dropped the keys in the
toilet. But that's what life is like. You're young, my Father says,
I'm not sure to me or Wang Wei, You don't understand

the world, the world which loves those who
enter it and then Wang Wei:

> Red hearts in the southern country
> Spring comes with stems enlarging.
> I didn't know you two were still together.

We're not, my Father says. He is unsentimental and gestures
at the wish that furnishes the mind of his son.
    Your son? asks Wang Wei. He has seen me and become real, as
though a ghost could die into a man. Not the monk you quite expect,
Wang Wei wears a cowboy's deadened face and stares
at you not unlike an establishing
shot. He says, Who are you?
    Like the scene in the movie, where the actors
find the camera and say Stop
looking at me, they quit the car and stand. And I say:

> Wish you'd gather some, caught me
> More of this thing that is longing.

And Wang Wei asks Who are you?
And my Father says Decide.

He is only waiting to die, my father tells my mother who tells me

    March into Grand Hotel while red fire flays it
    Pall-bearing waiters lay him on circular table
    He dead then why his lips still suck Marlboro Lights?

AT TAIPEI STATION, I SAW THIS CITY UNDRESS!

    Yes, he is dead and what can we do
    I met a man infected by English and he said please let me
        practice on you

My grandfather shuffles into the black alleyways
like a specter whose scene in the Act has ended
My eyes follow him as he steps on the floor tiles, black and chipped
    teeth
My grandfather says, *Come back in two years when I am eighty because I*
    will die then

Graffiti outside a fourth-floor University window. *Who kill my soul?*

    They have some problems stripping the veins from his chest but
        slowly
    he manages to crawl into

a glass jar that we slide into a birch box

His picture on the front

The hallway is walled with birch boxes

Living room lit by dimming cigarette:

Can I get you anything from California?

No.

He says in Chinese—This is only what will happen to everyone

Adjust your eyes to the unlit room.

ESSAY ON CRYING AT NIGHT

I am just like my mother. I buy books and tell myself that I am buying
wisdom and at the end of my life, I own a house full of books. When I
was little, I thought that the water came out of the showerhead
because it was crying. This is because I heard my mother crying and
thought it was the showerhead.

ECHO

"Such omissions of the subject allows the poet not
    to intrude his own personality upon the scene . . ."
    —James J. Y. Liu, *The Art of Chinese Poetry*

> *I can tell the wind is risin', leaves trembling on the tree,*
> *trembling on the tree.*

My father's father holding still, holding still a traffic jam of coughs

My father's mother steaming chicken, boiling soy and air

My mother's father dangling years—a broken pocket watch

My mother's mother bearing a wedding dress

My mother with such passion, sad beneath her silent face—frozen, a
    fashion ad

My father pressed in black and white—a single paper lantern pasted
    in the air beside him

I got to keep movin', I've got to keep movin'
Blues fallin' down like hail . . .

Faces that would not kiss in life
press together as the pages
close

Yeah standin' at the crossroad, tried to flag a ride
Ooo eeee, I tried to flag a ride
Didn't nobody seem to know me, babe, everybody pass me by

—though already in the future
ghosts roam through our dinner table
the steam from the vermicelli broth rising up like an apparition
Our knives and forks tick against our plates while we eat
I love her so much, but we haven't even met
I will cough my grandfather's cough and my
wife will smile with her mother's lips

THE YEAR-KILLER

We hired you first to bring our lives asceticism, some divine
subtraction to shave us down to our spirits, yet what you stole was our
senses. For how silly it sounded, paying a man to lessen us—and how
redundant, since we did pay you after all. We hired poorly, we
thought, since you started by making our life larger. You gave us
things: our friends whom we loved because they illuminated our lives
with stories, the discovery of favorite oldies and new foods, like the
mangosteen, that white womb-sack palmed inside an ox hoof, and
then our child and the stress of work. We enjoyed your fecund
mistake, marveling at how much you enlarged our days, until we
realized you were only beginning. You took my grandfather first and
then my mother, for which you gave me guilt in return. You took my
husband as well and I commanded you to stop. I realized then we
only command when we have no power to do so. I could not tell if
you obeyed for I found you had given me something—a calmness
that was either resignation or cynicism, I could not tell, and a

tiredness dabbed beneath my eyes. I did not feel sorry for myself. When you took me as well, I asked if your name was Time, but we both found it dishonest to personify this process of having and not having.

THERE ARE TWO TYPES OF TREES IN WINTER,

like my mother whose heart reveals itself opaquely, open as the outer
rings of an oak or the fifth doctor we see who says "Don't worry.
You're not going to die." Like my garrulous rash that tells my skin all
the secrets of my body or my younger brother who turns eleven today
and unhooks his PlayStation without saying anything so my Dad can
take him home to his mom, the windshield blackening when they
pull out as though dipped in chocolate. And our mutual loneliness is
like the purity of two trees, the dumb wood a cenotaph over these
moonlike snow months. The December night brushes over us like a
moth, the dark air more famished than sex, so use street lamp and car
window reflection—can you tell? Do my eyes look wet? Well, he
doesn't want to talk about it and the silence is the mystery he tracked
through pale familymist of Taiwan, detective's trail to locate the
suspect of himself—the past? We do not even know!

He asked about his parents, why they split up in the first place, what were they like when they were his age? My father—my mom's roommate from thirty years ago reveals—would mill around my mother's place every day, inspect the grass stubbling out of the street and wait for the moment to knock. He only had one good shirt and washed it every night in the bathroom sink. They don't talk about these things, my parents, who are as talkative as trees. Only two years ago, we inspect my father's father. We set aside our time with him as we would set a bone. His next performance: a failed rebuttal to death— sucking a Pall Mall and watching the news listless in his chair, slouching in a sullen wife-beater and baggy dress slacks. His grand-children, the way they look at him—as if merely by existing, we erect a history of regret ready to be lived ahead of us. One wonders how Batman feels about it, as he ponders the inevitable finale: Bruce Wayne bleeding on blue cave carpet. But does his cowl attest to an earlier death? Does that word offer a convenient name for the amethyst star blotting his face, his secret—identity? Sick outside of fictions, I read about it in a two-buck comic book, bed gabled with tissues and ineffable pox across my arms and torso. In Impressionism, all the characters are the same. Only the arrangement of the dots differs. Play with the slinky on my Dad's office desk. Take the AOL CD for a coaster. Turn on the newsradio for eight hours. The customer support girls gossip next door. And my Dad's e-mail after our first fight—"Like father and son. We are both too emotional, that is not good." We would drive home together, the traffic on 237 drifting up like incense towards the rust-subtle mountains.

This was when we talked. Summer we shared the morning commute like a tiny chair and is it autumn already, when the fourth doctor says, "My friend, you're what we like to call a fun patient—we can't quite figure out what's wrong with you." But it used to keep us up, my sister and I kept up all night by my father on the phone with his girlfriend, his voice startling to hear. After breakfast, he opens the pantry and takes pills for hypertension, high blood pressure, LDL cholesterol, and angina. We never talked about it. We pretended we were dumb and forgetful and maybe it was better that way—not like this dumb rash's dotty autographs. At the doctor's office, I watch the doctor's wall. A new flu bulletin! Have good posture! No one in my family got sick not in that way at least. My grandmother didn't call when her stomach bled. Calling would wake my mom. What can you really say about it? He couldn't talk at the funeral and I envy the trees, who know no sentiment. Not branches. Roots burying themselves always into the earth. My Father tells my brother to shut up. The waiter at Jade Pavilion thinks my mother is my sister. The waiter walks up and says, "It doesn't matter that no one is home, we still love her." He pours the tea and asks, "What good is eternal youth if no one loves you?"

She takes me to the last doctor. Doctor number seven. Who jerks his finger in the air and says "Ah, Penicillin! Penicillin muddies the waters!" and his hair plugs rustle like a lawn in suburbia. Laughing at my red rash, he expostulates, "It's just an allergic reaction." The greedy mapmaker owned no kingdom, the mirror no image.

"Nothing serious." Not my mother alone in Taipei for the first time in years, sad quest for the custody of my sister. Not my father telling us to sit down and behave ourselves, as we view his father ceasing to exist. Not the time I refused to go to law school and my father walked away, only time I've ever seen him evasive, sits at his desk and—I don't understand what are you saying. Did I force you. Did I say you have to. Did I put a knife to your throat. When autumn turns winter, the snow covers us into secrets. There are two types of trees in winter. Deciduous, Evergreen. We never talked about it. We talked about it. This is how plants prepare for winter. Last day of work, after he lived with his father all summer, he held the front door open. "Okay Dad I'm leaving now I'll see you but (and now his voice begins to crack!) I don't know when I'll see you." His father looks up from the kitchen table and says "It's okay. Go see your mother."

ANTI-TANTALUS

. . . and the desert invaded. The tall black sands, a dusty film,

lairs of bric-a-brac, junk thrust upon us—a flooding wall.

We ran, we ran from the songs of cities bared.

We ran and deserted the familiar look that the world owns, the future
   we had booked,

traded for this tapering mess of clouds and moss, flowers and figures
   through doors.

The streets cast off their apparent face, leaving floating lights,
   sirens—no bodies but fedoras and black coats,

a strange breed, the sort of man from Magritte, immigrating inside
   you, or a pulp film

where the full ripened grain of black and white pours up the wall:

villain masked, unknown; hero unfound; dame desired, but dead in
   the end (fade-out blurs her body bared).

These bodies—these landmarks—a desert to us, evaporating like the
   shadows of friends from books—
They are what occupy us, boarders sliding letters under our door.
These are the fluid emissions of the self, the lava of influence. Where
   am I in this black pea coat?
There is sand in my mouth—strands of saliva in a freckled sheet of
   film.

   You are all free,
   free to enter, free to leave. The movie stammers off and it is here
   that we commence the trading routes. I am tainted by your
      more plain venoms—
   jokes, insights, chit chat, concern.
   We begin to converse—empire of gestures and laughs.

   Commerce always. We are givers.
   We are takers, our shadows
   having no choice but to overlap.

DRAMATIC MONOLOGUE AGAINST THE SELF

Hello, my name is Ken Chen. For my essay today, the organizers of this panel have procured a microphone named _____. Although this microphone may resemble and is a person, it is I who would like to discuss essays and how essays permit us to become the microphones of others. I enjoy being a microphone because I enjoy hearing the thoughts of others. I believe the essay is a genre of performance, which is not voice, but the author's mind bending a thought like gravity influencing the curvature of light. We find ourselves bored by creative nonfiction, autobiography, and memoir, which forsake the personality of thought for the impersonality of narrative. We sit in the essay as in a room of normal talk, free from aesthetics, stripped until we are only selves, struggling to unhide the strangeness of our souls!—Well to be honest I don't know if I buy this. The way I see it, an essay makes you helpless, you're suffocated. It's one mind all the way down. And yes, if the goal of the essay is to televise cognition, then the essay has no room for discreteness, because the mind itself knows no walls. But it is this openness that makes essays difficult to write and exceptionally good items of luggage. We can snare the world into them. The great alternative novels, such as *Moby-Dick, Tristram Shandy,* and *In Search of Lost Time,* are hauls of essays, revealing an oblique characteristic of our experimental literature—its discursiveness. Consider the essaylike qualities of—and here he goes on to list a bunch of names, what a ridiculous namedropper! The essay, by virtue of being everywhere, never sequesters itself in one place. For this reason, however much the essay is our habit, the regional headquarters for our thinking, it is also a lawless form. It looks like he goes off on some weird tangent here about how he'd write literary criticism by conducting fake interviews. He would play the part of a buffoonish professor and improvise answers to questions his friend would ask by AOL Instant Messenger. These questions would guide the conversation towards certain topics, occasionally forcing Mr. Chen to explain certain weaknesses in his position, but the back-and-forth of the interview actually fried them—fried them? That must be a typo. Freed them. And if I were present, if I were truly and corporeally there, I would adjust my glasses and testify that the essay is our only medium still in love with subject matter, that it is a naïve art, that out of all our literary genres, it is our most popular and marginal, two adjectives that explain rather than contradict each other. Unlike lyric poetry, the essay remains a medium rather than a genre, a tool rather than art. We have not yet honed this box of commentary into a delicate pocket square. We still let the essay subtract us with questions. Yet to say that the essay questions suggests that it quests. The essay may wander, it may be a science of associations, but it wanders with a goal. We say, *Look, a thought!* And along we scurry holding a dish to catch it. Coughs.

STAGE DIRECTIONS

I would prefer that the audience believe these interruptions to be authentic. However, if the reader of this essay feels uncomfortable pretending to trespass, then this disclaimer may be read prior to the actual essay itself—preserving the aesthetic effect of the interruption, but not the subversiveness of it.

TAIPEI NOVEL

She said to her husband, "Last night
my life was so quiet that my feelings were audible.
When the phone rang, I thought it was my heart."

They met at a weeklong conference in Taipei, a city neither thought to
enjoy. Neither of them spoke the language, except when they
dreamed.

She dreamed the hotel bartender served her
a shot glass in which her heart glowed and floated. If they had not
gone drinking, she would never have told him that
she had cheated on her husband.

Look at the sky. . . . Someone has
broken a tooth of ice
and called it the moon.

Look at this glass. Look at her uncontroversial face. Its dimensions are two inches by four inches. We commonly use it for drinking. At the continental breakfast each morning, she ate milk and bread, the clichés of food. She was lonely and perfect, if we do not count her self.

❖

> "I like eating with him because he knows
> my secret. Even though we do not
> talk about my secret."

They ditched the conference. They visited the night markets at Shilin and Huahsi. They visited the National Palace Museum. They visited the Grand Hotel. They visited sites that further description would debase into fragrance. They hated the humidity and visited the Ambassador Theater, which was air conditioned, and watched *Top Gun*. Their hatred for *Top Gun* was commensurate with their hatred of humidity, so they began swimming in the hotel pool. They noted how easily they hated things. She was afraid to swim because of the lightning and watched him and chatted with him, amused by his humorless joy and his earnestness, illustrated by his purchase of Confucius's *Analects,* which he believed would help him "understand the natives." When they were in the Cineplex, she touched his knee, for which they both felt guilty.

"Bright and dark we fall asleep in the movie theater."

He looked at her wrist, his eyes exhausted
by looking at her.

These small quick moons
running across before the light changes.

He lay on the rocks. "I watched her watch
the fishing lamps."

"When I am alone, I feel penitent, my heart damp like cold metal."

❖

Out it tumbles, hot, scalding, mixed, marvelous, terrible, oppressive!

Would it be melodramatic to say the sex terrified him? It solved his
insomnia, not by dissolving wakefulness but by replacing it. He
began to dream he was a wolf.

"I remember him staring out the window at the highway." She
rose from the bed and saw the moon tug the fur thistles from his
skin, a magnet drawing out steel shavings. She saw his face—dark,
but also gentle, just least gentle to himself.

Confucius: The Odes can be summed up in one phrase—Swerve
not from the right path. (II.2)

Wolf: This is why I have a global positioning system.

The light orange against
the branches.
A lamp-lit brain.

A man, a woman
A mirror.

As each day passes, the moon dims up and
down like a heartbeat.

❖

Sky dark as nuzzling faces.
He thought love was a room that power could not enter.
"It wasn't like that. I was lonely then."
A new relationship makes detectives of all of us.
What if the heart is no one's goal. What if it is an outcome.

"I stretch the blanket to a triangle.
I turn slowly to the wall. I have begun to know
this wall."

❖

He has done nothing but swim
in the last few days—
swimmer who drinks up a lake to turn blue.

And the waters swallow him—are like the tears you shed.

Then he must not be swimming, for there were no tears;

❖

"I saw a mitten on the sidewalk and burst into tears."

Always walk by her
house at night. Music but
no lights.

The car in the barren lot.

The wet stars dipped in water.

Two dents in
her garden. His feet
are dirty.

Staring at power lines over pale lawn chairs—

The light cast by the reflections from the pool

❖

How does everything seem so peaceful suddenly?

This calm tender state, where it is not impermissible to be yourself.

He would have described love as the rumor that fills the world.

❖

He did not remember his dreams, having no one to tell them to when he woke.

> *Confucius:* How I have gone downhill! It has been such a long time since I have dreamt of the Duke of Chou. (VII.5)

> Hello rose. Hello bone.
> Hello touchtone cellular phone.
> Let the kettle
> whistle all night long. Let the water boil while it sings.

When he asked his secretary why he didn't have enough Continuing
Education credits, he learned that he had neglected to register at the
conference in Taipei.

Reading his copy of *The Analects,* she found it alternately funny and
impenetrable.

Yet still she looked away from other men.

Years later, she is at a party.
Wine stain on new dress.
Sweaty hands oiling the crystal glass.
"Who is the figure I spot across the room? What
is this voice I hear, this voice
walking towards me?"

Confucius (by the river): What passes away is, perhaps, like this. Day
and night it never lets up. (IX.17)

2.   **BANAL LOVE SONGS**

Tonight, when we were halfway to nakedness,
the loneliest place for *Don't*—

THE MANSIONS OF THE MOON

The crescent fattened, making content the anorexic moon.
Escapes the smog and eats the road, the moon winds up
our time and chews the road back into itself. The moon is
tattooed by black pattern of branch. The moon is shy
and hides like two people behind a silence and pretense
of no emotion. It understands what it is like
to have one's own heart carved away in phases.
This is the price of being
other than lifeless.
An eyelid goes gibbous with water.
For a frozen moment, the moon
has sunk into a sphere, the perfect solid of memory—
all thoughts equidistant from the soul,
the thought-light focusing on
two humans together, growing alone.

YES, NO, YES, THE FUTURE, GONE, HAPPY, YES, NO, YES, CUT, YOU

The first sentence of this poem is not about you.

    In this respect, it is unlike the last sentence and my heart.

Is the heart a thing that can be about something?

    We were about

    to break up and after that, we broke up.

Did it have to end in this—I mean, was there anything

else I could have done?

    See fifth-to-last sentence.

When dinner wilts into memory,

when the frost florescent bars in parking lots

spangle out like bones blooming from a tree,

when I busy myself out towards sleep, wheel around,

adorned-in by alone from every direction,

when the moon outdopples the ambulance siren and the evening

pollutes itself with reference, suffused by our lost

elbow-clasping smoky-tender moist and utmost shirtless plucked-up
  naked nights—
when I miss you, does that make the first sentence false?
  Because I think about you more now that
  my life no longer mentions you.
If statement is when
antecedent and consequent clap their hands: having thought
for a while, having understood
what we have built behind us, let me ask
what is the wilderness
charring the scene before me?
  It is called the future, the branches feathery
  and lowing in the wind.
Now call the consequent a painting and why don't I see you in this
  painting?
  Now that you are no longer here, a scar floats as halo
  above my scalp and when you come back, I grow jealous
  of your talents.
What are my talents?
  You are so good at being happy, a skill I too
  practice (or try to practice) and despise.
Well, don't worry—I've been to the future and seen that scar
evaporate into a crown. Will you call me in September?
  The conversation was boring—fat pauses like
  lakes and I didn't know what to say.

Did I want to hang up?

    No, never. I must have loved you.

Are questions like relationships?

    Questions have answers, unless they are questions nine or two.

What are questions for?

    One can use a question mark for many things. For example: as a
        sickle for cutting people's hearts off.

How can you cut someone off with a question?

    You know, like when I said, "Yeah, but we're still in love with
        each other, right?" and you told me the answer.

ADVERSARIAL

1. Even if God, who possesses infinite time and proficiency, read every work of literature, he would still lack a neutral position from which to evaluate the texts. He would find his adjudication tainted by the unavoidable task of reading the books *in sequence*. My disputant replied that a creature as impossible as God would find little problem reading every single work after every other one, including itself.

2. "Indeed, one of the most important books of Abelard, *Sic et Non* (*Yes and No*), merely documents by successive quotations a list of over 150 inconsistencies and discrepancies in the Bible and in the writings of the church fathers and other authorities, assuming them all to be true and leaving it to the reader to try to harmonize them." Harold J. Berman, *Law and Revolution: The Formation of the Western Legal Tradition.*

And when we found each other under the lake and when we held each other under that lake and had he air, he would have whispered *Am I drowning and can I drown some more?* In our bog of bed, washed up and sweat-hot, my heart began the timid beat boxing when I spoke your name, wet name that conquers down into my throat and woke your dozing heart. The day is drying to meet you! So, squeeze the lime-sun and pour yourself on this nail and we shall dance together, in spite of my allergies. Drag yourself by the hair to the motel where our future selves fuck forgot to make reservations it's okay we'll sleep in the station wagon, thriving in our own way, not nostalgic for when we first met. Waited three days to present ourselves barefoot in the snow and confess. Night coming, we wade slow towards our cold milkfresh star, the eyelid theater that intrudes on sleep, the mix CDs and Polaroids—tender proof of all our past! Neither of us knows how the story will end, except that it is morning and we have just been born, our hearts ladled with larks, no—sparrowsong and NPR drenching the cool apartment, you kissing my eyes while I pretend I'm still asleep.

Last night, I saw Maurice Pialat's *Van Gogh* and was struck by a scene in which a thirteen-year-old girl tells van Gogh that food is better than painting. If he stops painting, she says, he will live. If he stops eating, he will die. I thought about this and decided that it was an unfair comparison. Although food is more necessary than painting, each painting on its own is less replaceable. We may be required to eat, but it matters little what we eat so long as we participate in the general activity of food.

I told my neighbor about this scene and reasoned further that if we stop painting, we will live, but if we do not love one another, we will die.

My neighbor disagreed, on the basis that my ex was not "The One."

I replied that everyone is "The One" because everyone is unique.

He thought for a moment and replied: "The germane analogy for the lover is not painting, but food. If everyone is equally unique, then everyone is equally replaceable."

BON VOYAGE, OUR SWELTERING US!

He spent last night staring at the bathroom mirror, as though waving his reflection goodbye and waiting for himself to leave. Five blocks away, she walks down the street and the wind blows her hair into her eyes. She parts it out of the way. These things have nothing in common with each other except that they have nothing in common with each other.

LONG DISTANCE LOVE — CAN IT WORK?

Is that why you never want me anymore?
Holding this book to my face, I did not speak.
What do you call this book?
I do not call it a mirror for the romantic, though there is someone
    looking
at us even now! What would it mean to cure the heart
its metaphysick? Curing is a
salting process to preserve dead meat. What do you call it
when you sit staring abandoned, hand scrubbing elbow and
    wondering?
I am not lonely. I am too far
from the world—in fact, nearly a foot separates
the mind from the heart, these two meats already resting
on the flower-inlaid porcelain dinner plate.
That mumbling you hear—*Pudomt Lahdom Bubum!*—
is my heart singing its intimate song, that coughing red crumb!

Slippery in your hands, my heart shudders like a gasping fish.

You have such beautiful hands.

The medieval Chinese figured the heart as the organ of the mind,

which would mean that there was no distance

and reminds me—

I discovered today the antidote to temptation.

Oh really!

Not restraint but narrow distances.

(Oh I see where this is going.)

So I'd rather not know you, I told myself. This was a convenient

decision. We'd been separated a year.

Why do you always joke around when you feel vulnerable?

What would you have me do?

Deploy your heart past its range. That sound

is not the heart beating. It stammers.

The goal of love is to be unmastered.

This meat is still alive!

"LOVE IS LIKE TAUTOLOGY IN THE SAME WAY *LIKE* IS LIKE TAUTOLOGY"

Love is like tautology in the same way *like* is like tautology. Both are technologies with which we can turn one thing into another. *Like* for example turns an object around until we realize that what we had thought was a moon had actually been something else entirely—a pearl perhaps—and that the pearl was white because it had contained an ocean of jade-white waves, though this ocean's true identity was a tear, which some tend to liken to a moon. Love too is about turns. It begins with turning my head to meet your eye and ends when I turn away from you, lost, our hearts split rather than won. The middle of love—when we forget that love is what describes us—occurs when I turn to you for everything: to learn how to sleep, to remind myself that yes I too possess a body and slowly it seems life conveys forward only so I have something to tell you at dinner. Time passes and I know you so well that these two terms—I and You (henceforth, "U")— grow indivisible, are the same—are tautological. Friendship is an expression; love is an equation.

Yet even equations can be unhappy. The problem arises when the letters are miswritten, when I = X as in an ex-love interest who wishes to change from an ex to a U. Say that S and E fall (collapsing like a weak will) in front of X and we will say that these letters spell out the problem. Or say that you find a letter written from X to I and U asks Why? Why are you doing this to me? Why do you have to talk to her—to X? (Let X be the ex-sex.) U asks you this on the phone, when I (by which I mean I) calls and says that he will come home late tonight. I imagines that U is sitting in a nightgown or the hallway—yes, she's pacing back and forth in the hallway, her hands shaking, and there are moments on the phone when U says nothing and even I know that she's only trying to not sound like someone who is crying. But I, however, realizes that U *is* someone who is crying and remember that he *is* I—and not X and is therefore U, which is another way of saying that I did not remember I loved you until you started crying. This is the problem with thinking in letters: letters can be variable but love must be constant.

If love and *like* are both like equal signs, then is love like *like?* There are times when we mean to say *I love you* (represented variously by *I love U* and *I love X*), but sometimes this is too difficult or maybe I just don't feel like saying that kind of thing on the phone—especially when U sounds like she's crying—and instead we say *I like you,* because we tell ourselves that *like* is not that different from love—that the two may even be interchangeable. The moon loves a pearl. I like X. These are statements of varying degrees of incorrectness: first, the moon cannot love a pearl because the moon is a satellite, an inanimate rock lacking the emotional landscape required for love; secondly, while it is true that I occasionally like X, I think I am far more like U. It's true.

I call you up to tell you this, but no one answers the phone. Should I go home to see you? I do. There is no U. I is only me, me without you. There is a word for this. When there is only I, when I equals I— we call this an identity. I sit on the couch and wait for you to come back. I get bored and watch TV. I fall asleep. When I get up, it occurs to me you're not here. For no reason at all I go to the kitchen and start randomly opening the cabinets so that I might find you. I can't remember what I was looking for and close the cabinets back up. I like you more than X—no, I love you and not X. I wanted to tell you this but you're not here and I'm not the same me who spoke to you on the phone so I can't really say it then and I realize I also like you more than I like I. I like telling you what my day is like more than I like telling myself what my day is like. I go to the bathroom and come back and turn off the TV. I forget it is off and stare at it for no reason.

HEARTBREAK IS A LEAK OF SELF.

Tonight, I plugged the cracks under my door.

When I told him
I missed you even when I was asleep, he said Sleep
next to a grandfather clock. When you said, I've been having trouble
sleeping lately, did you really mean—The rain is the typist
of my dreams?

Even the ceiling is crying tonight!

IT IS A CITY YOU SEE THROUGH WATER

Stranger. SEA–TAC 5.58 PM SAT

When I woke up
you served on a silver tray—an omelet and condom. All night
we had looked at each other and thought Who are you? 9.45 AM SUN

The wet lamplight tangles into wire. It will
stitch your eyes closed. YOUR APARTMENT WINDOW 6.01 PM SUN

shifted 9.30 PM FRI

light. FLYING 9.06 PM SUN

woke up, 9.45 AM SUN

as an I 2.24 PM SAT

a small 5.31 PM SUN

Seattle—it seems to have almost nothing 5.57 PM SUN

The bus hinges when it turns, as an *I* becomes a letter *L*, as in "We are lodged
within the bus's folds." I put my head on your shoulder and think of when
you called two weeks ago and said, *I am only calling to tell you we are not going out. That
is all I have to say and goodbye.* SANDPOINT BUS 2.24 PM SAT

to do with you. 5.57 PM SUN

Art and no one else at the abandoned Naval park.

This week's *Stranger*

plastered red on the asphalt, soaked with the

blood from your scraped knee. SEA–TAC 5.56 PM SUN

(I am sitting in the shuttle. My hands smell like 10.30 PM SUN

no idea why." YOUR APARTMENT 5.26 PM SUN

The heart TAXI WINDOW 5.31 PM SUN

In 9.39 PM FRI

flight. 9.30 PM FRI

In 9.39 PM FRI

coldly TAXI TO SEA–TAC 5.30 PM SUN

coldly 5.30 PM SUN

Berkeley

and Seattle STANDING IN OAK CAR LOT 9.40 PM FRI

a couple shivering with 10.27 PM SUN

wet 6.01 PM SUN

eyes closed. 6.01 PM SUN

is a city you see through water. 5.31 PM SUN

A grandmother and her daughter stop

at North Oakland. At Hoyt, another boy to his I-Pod leashed.

It is not sentimental to return home. I see a couple shivering with their dog.

SHUTTLE FROM OAK 10.27 PM SUN

My feet step out into the street EXITING SHUTTLE 10.56 PM SUN

My feet step out into the street 10.56 PM SUN

And the stewardess says my baggage may have shifted in flight. 9.30 PM FRI

The 6.01 PM SAT

dog. 10.27 PM SUN

light. FLYING 9.06 PM SUN

stitch YOUR APARTMENT WINDOW 6.02 PM SAT

blood, SEA–TAC 5.56 PM SAT

going out. BUS 2.30 PM SAT

! 5.23 PM SUN
i

We played *Mario Kart* and you wanted to win.

You did win but only by tickling me. YOUR LIVING ROOM 3 PM SAT

This place FLYING 9.06 PM SUN

This place you happen to live with, I realize this city

is not made of rain. It's made of 9.06 PM SUN

is not sentimental 10.27 PM SUN

like you.) 10.30 PM SUN

away from 2.24 PM SAT

I see your apartment window coldly lit

like a small rectangular

moon TAXI TO SEA–TAC 5.30 PM SUN

The cab!

You sat at the mattress edge and said, *You are*

leaving and I have no idea why. YOUR BEDROOM 5.23 PM SUN

And you did win YOUR LIVING ROOM 3 PM SAT

put my head on your shoulder and think 2.24 PM SAT

step out into the street 10.56 PM SUN

stop 10.27 PM SUN

And why did I think that we could not understand? 5.24 PM SUN

Small rectangular TAXI TO SEA-TAC 5.30 PM SUN

halted 5.30 PM SUN

heart 5.24 PM SUN

From above FLYING 9.04 PM SUN

Berkeley and STANDING IN OAK CAR LOT 9.40 PM FRI

halted a little in orbit. TAXI TO SEA–TAC 5.30 PM SUN

this FLYING 9.05 PM SUN

those BUS 2.24 PM SAT

shivering OAK CAR LOT 9.42 PM SUN

hinges BUS 2.24 PM SAT

leashed SHUTTLE FROM OAK 10.27 PM SUN

THE CITY OF HABITS

When you speak of how poorly I treat you, you speak as though we have a thing inside us, such as a heart, a mind, or other flint ball that we strike with our thoughts and spark into intentions. I do not believe that we have intentions. We possess practices, an ecosystem of habits that may or may not be good for us. The dew on the grass stalks, the air-moistening leaf and the dark and breathing woods—our lush habits give us a life that we can breathe before we dive back into the black waters. We spend most our lives in these waters.

The lovers, intense, passionate, keep getting lost

Tonight, pearled with high-beams, the cars escorting couples to their lives—unstarred night since you were at Howe Street and I was walking home.

The headlights—not a car, but two motorcycles.

A man who congratulates himself before a couple for introducing the two of them. But he did not introduce them to each other and in fact they have just broken up.

Commute home.
Williamsburg Bridge.
How does the bridge implicate us?

How lovely to be modern, when the entire world is inanimate!

The couple bought a furnished apartment, but the day before they moved in, the landlord sent movers to switch the expensive furniture for the cheap.

How the snow silts outside my window, bricking our apartment into an egg. Sorry, my apartment.

He studies the ceiling for hours before he sleeps—for the ceiling is ours.
He wore the bedroom ceiling as his eyelid.

Sadness, the cave—Have fun burying yourself!

The birds alight at our feet and begin to burrow into dirt.

He found it difficult to recognize beauty. Honest enough his sadness not beautiful.

Longing would be so much easier without the other person obstructing it.

I believe you discuss romantic loss because it allows you to believe that you are an innocent person who must merely solve a problem that is small, temporary, and local.

In love, that holy toy.

Just because you are the victim does not mean that you are not the perpetrator.

❖

She is excited to see his friends but when she gets to the bar finds that he is fighting with them and slinks away.

She wanted to talk to the fantastic man who'd help her understand all the answers. And he did know the answer to every question. Just not the correct one.

The fantasy being the existence of the answer.

Caravan of yellow lights—the drive-thru after ten.

Why do we cover our mouths in embarrassment? Once we have seen the fangs we can never forget them.

❖

The woman who once upon a time decided to eat no food and breathe no air, so she would let nothing more inside herself.

Though she turns up the radio so his neighbors will think she has guests, she is aware that the walls are too thick for them to eavesdrop.

From her garden, she grew radios that played only at night.

Your neighbors having sex
The drill of pencil sharpening
The white chorus of stars
The bodies hurdling over railing one-by-one
This alarm will not stop ringing though it makes no noise!

❖

A woman tying her shoelaces.

The interoffice intercom interrupted her daydreams and uttered nothing, since its injunction was internal.

Afterwards, she developed a crush on her coworker, which allowed her to procrastinate on love, since after all, there he was.

Miserable angels, civilians, and office assistants—to build a soul, you must lather yourself with past. The stone star attracts debris around it. It lights the footsteps that flame on the asphalt before you. Time falls while you slept.

❖

Good night and then Tetris and morning tea.

Yesterday's mail on the table: Tribe Called Quest t-shirt, Chekhov paperback, toothbrush, her earring.

No note.

Because he had become an adult, he no longer improvised.

Your face when telling stories you are satisfied with. Your face when bored as if your soul had fallen asleep. Your face when everything falls off it—honest face. The vault of your looks is burning. Stare as I grease the air, watch my sweet arson until all that remains is a charred mark denting the grasses.

through toy ruins, bitten-off tiles
slurred rafters

He imagined the stone star to be only a large die thrown down by God, so often that it wore down its corners.

The nature of a die is that it forgets your last throw, but the misery you face is merely the latest iteration of all the miseries on your list.

To die—the motivational threat. Here is the wall of fire. We shall do what we can as we wait for it to incinerate us.

The love that came up to you and said "No longer be who you are."

❖

Since the separation was irrevocable, the enemy was hope.

Which left him with a nihilistic joy.

He imagined the top of a blank page that said: See God, *supra,* who called you into his office with the sunny eastern exposure to reality, gazed upon his creation, and said *Stet!*

That night on our way back from the beach when we drove through the orchard lit by tangerines and the streetlamps powdered rice upon the asphalt and we found ourselves feathered by the moonshine—that night you said it feels like we're onstage. This morning I figured out who our audience was.

These experiences taught me how to tell myself a story without realizing it and slowly begin to uninterpret it to myself.

We found the missing world inside a brownstone, which you will notice, has no floors. The walls and windows circumscribe the white boulder which rolls in place in the air. Walk on it and learn the purpose of the earth revolving.

The earth is a millstone that sharpens us into saint.

My life is not unbearable yet still I must escape it.

IN THE CITY I DROWNED ALL NIGHT IN

THE NOTHING SEARCH FOR YOU.

I found your pajamas folded on the sidewalk, your nylons glossing
the bare branches transparent.
I still find your little notes in my books, your hairs
when I change the bed sheets.

You-clues everywhere.

EVAPORATE

Can you believe

we were strangers once, dry

and unhatched, the future waiting over us like a pool?

June burst the blue sack

of rain and we huddled downstreet under ruined umbrella.

You threw

a bottle at my roof at two AM. I hid Dunhills

in your pocket, the smog sky singing a lunar tune.

Tonight, the rain unspools.

The rain taps the nightlong glass desperate,

begging to be let in.

Well, let me moisten you with time, until the wet embalms us.

Let love flood us its lucky era.

Let this wet epoch soak the bedroom till our necks

wear lakes for collars.

The lifeguard states—Do not allow anyone of any age

to swim alone; drowning occurs
to adults too—and now the waters kiss us to the roof!
That time we kissed each other all night, did we
hickey the redless flesh-juiced time out of us
or were we just trying to wet each other
into pure duration?
Our pink exhalations steam towards the sky,
yet I find myself startled
by the emptied room, as you too evaporate.
Dawn chalks its blooming line.
We were immortal once, but look now at my skin
wrinkling into marble.
Morning, the world's white roof,
warms the waters we accrued.
The rain dries upward.
This bedroom, this drained moat.

3.   THE INVISIBLE MEMOIR

My gold sword sunk into ground.

My spirit lost among the long weeds.

Then in the cool night. Then in the quiet sky. Then the moon
    blossoming open.

My mind goes back to those old hallways, but now only

the light glows hollow on the waters of Ch'in-huai.

Uncle's house—the happiest time of my life.

Staying—fate

3rd daughter

Grandfather—divorce

Your son is having an affair

The same price

I pay for the son, you pay for the daughter

Mother's father and mother
Father's mother and father
Mother and father
Sister

The tears of Chinese mermaids are said to be pearls.

I think their coming here affect our marriage.

My mother and I are sitting in a café in Cupertino, eating *bao bing*.
"If Li Yu had put into governing his state the effort
that he put into composing poetry, he would never
have become my prisoner!"
Alternatively referred to as beautiful island, northern outpost, and the
Gates of Hell.

Dad and the two houseguests

I sit with my sister on my grandmother's couch, where we stare at the
coffee table and chew dried sour plums and wafers of Chinese candy,
like a pink roll of pennies. My mother would measure our height
against our grandmother, who with her husband had fled Beijing for
Taipei and then San Jose after my parents had settled in California.
When my mother was homesick, she thought of Taiwan, unlike her
mother who thought of China. My grandmother had acquired a

patience that wanted nothing—a sort of contented despair. Because she and my grandfather were Christian, they did not celebrate holidays such as The Ghost Month, when the gates of hell are said to open. The great sorrow of decapitation as opposed to strangulation is that the body will appear in the realms below without a head. The family of any condemned man who may have sufficient means will always bribe the executioner to sew it on again.

—I didn't know you lived with her parents
—I did?

    I.   Creating a world. Consider Proust, Bellow, Renoir. What is a detail?

    II.   No theory of Chinese culture or citations of Classical Chinese poetry and folk tales.

    III.   Problem of Chinese language. No reproduction of calligraphy or etymology of Chinese characters. Language becomes white space when the main character does not understand it.

IV.   Against authenticity. If the exotic is the sensuous enigma, no sensuousness. Zero lyricism of food, night markets, Chinese customs, nature. No use of the appositive, the clause that annotates a noun (e.g., "the clause that annotates a noun").

V.   Fate is a trap, but context is dynamic.

Before we got married
Making our way through the weeping willows, singing
Crying on the plane leaving Taipei
The year he born, the military police had already taken up
positions when the demonstrators had arrived
The fall wind in the garden. The moss taking over the steps.
The screen hanging beaded over the closed door—
Why open it. Who comes.

Outside the curtains: Sa Sa, the sound
of rain. Spring is almost over. These silk blankets
are too thin, the fifth watch too cold
and in my dream, I had forgotten
about all of this—my self, this exile.

Again in pleasure.
I am starting to think—that when the sun
is setting and you are resting alone, it's better not
to look south to those streams and hills. Leaving
them was easy—but going back last night
was hard. The waters flowing away. The flowers
breaking to the ground. Spring has also left.
    That heaven, this earth.

Don't gossip
Live in the past

REGARDING THE AUTOBIOGRAPHICAL SOURCES OF LI YU'S VERSE

Li Yu (also known as Li Hou Zhu, 937–978), the last ruler of the
Southern Tang Dynasty, is the inventor of the confessional voice in
Chinese lyric poetry. His oeuvre, which is conventionally read as
autobiographical, portrays a young man in love with his wife, his
subsequent lamentations over her death, and his eventual exile as a
failed king, political prisoner, and widower in the Song capital, where
he was murdered. The famously romantic account of Li's death holds
that the Song ruler poisoned him after he wrote a poem that grieved
the loss of his kingdom and protested the rape of his second wife by a
Song nobleman.

—How did the two of you select him for your translations?

—It was my mother's decision.

However, it is equally possible that Li died of chronic illness. And it is also curious that almost all of his thirty-seven surviving poems are impossible to place accurately in the chronology of his life. And while these poems depict a devastating nostalgia for one's home, this itself was a conventional period motif; in fact the poems were titled after the popular melodies to which they were sung.

—When I was a girl at my uncle's house in *Yi-Lan*
Put on a play every night. Singing, dancing.

One uses one phrase for one thing (Taipei) and these guests (wet door of stainless steel, smog moist over weeping willows) wait behind the door that is each word.

Well what would you call it. I thought they traded you.

No they just dumped me.

Sometimes they make this decision and suffer.

Adopted

Maybe it was better this way

His sister.

The time of return.

Raised by Grandma (paternal)

Medicine too expensive

Laughter – she was an ugly baby

She had a different name there

"If you see an old lady, call her Obasan!"

Taiwan *baba*

Baba che

The way the girl is outgoing in Chinese

Come here let me tell you something since he can't understand

We invented ghosts to hide the thing from its definition. We miss the thing, which was not lovable, he was stingy and spoke a Mandarin that smelled like nicotine, who gave us candy when we sat on her couch, and who worked as a statistician when he was in Beijing—but the thing itself no longer exists. "Tomorrow, my mother will be dead," wrote Jules Renard in 1900. "I shall know another ghost." Pu Song-Ling, the author of the Ming Dynasty classic *Liaozhai Zhiyi* (*Strange Tales from a Chinese Studio*), describes a man named Hsu who carries the ghost of his true love and finds her "so light that she is like carrying a child." When translator Herbert Giles compares this "to the German notion that the spirit of the dead mother, coming back at night to suckle the child she has left behind, makes an impress on the bed alongside the baby," we may argue that he divulges an appositive desire—the desire to contextualize. While Giles aims only to renovate the scope of the sentence, widening his focus from a Chinese romance to a nursing mother in Germany, it seems also accurate to say that he describes the weight of the past as it hangs behind each object, thick and transparent. The appositive is the noun's ghost.

Father heart attack
—Felt like someone pressing their palm on my chest
Friends said it'll go away. We should just pray
(I try to speak. *Don't try too hard. We know all about your limitations.*
Yeah you have a big mouth)
Sit down and pray

Frequently occurring words in Li Yu

Spring (27)

One, Blossom, Dream, Not (20)

Wind, Moon (18)

Person (10)

No words my own, nothing to say, climbing alone

    the western chamber. The moon bent like a hook.

Lonely under the sycamores—all autumn, locked in . . .

    Cannot cut it cleanly off or even

order it without the mess. This is

    the sorrow of leaving—no other taste in my heart.

Which, well cooked, are a very good substitute for asparagus.

I think we become adults when we cannot explain our life to anyone without using appositives.

Last night: wind and rain against the curtains,

   Sa, Sa—the sound of fall.

The wick is out, the fifth watch finished

   but I am still thinking, propped up by this pillow, thinking.

The days fall slowly out of this world, water from a river.

   My life wavering as though inside a dream.

The only stable road is to the wine rack.

   Otherwise, why walk.

The trip? It was different than I thought

More comical

     I.   Arrival

           a. We have to walk along the outer edge

           b. Uncle seems hesitant to hug us

           c. Description of *Yi-Ma, Yi-Fu*

     II.   Car ride

           a. I sit in the back, exhausted, not civil

           b. Everyone thinks I'm an idiot. I'm tired. I can't speak Chinese. Sitting in the back. I can't believe I'm here.

III. Apartment
   a. Motorcycles, red doors, green sans serif lettering on mailbox
   b. Elephant-headed coat racks, water cooler only hot and warm water, picture of a praying girl made out of beads, Chinese wall painting.
IV. Johnny
   a. Does Kenny have a mole? Mosquito
   b. I've missed you
   c. Jackie Chan
   d. Massage—the mom planned the date of engagement—the rush
V. The next morning
   a. We decide to take a walk
      i. My mother's blouse
      ii. Pink everywhere
      iii. Mom pointing out Starbucks, Domino's pizza
      iv. Sugarcane
      v. Taking pictures
      vi. Argument about shirts
      vii. Chinese foreshortening
      viii. Death when you stop being the artist of your context. You become context
      ix. Notes on wedding
      x. Notes on funeral

1963

When she walked home from middle school in the early sixties, the
   path to the train
cut through the red light district where you could eat anything.
Acrobats, prostitutes.
Through the rice fields where she swore she saw a ghost.
I want to go back
Premonitions of tragedy
Only a mini-mall!

1977

Taiwan Ambassador at next table
So asked him to marry us on the spot

2006

Jet-lagged, dozing at wedding banquet
Crying
Taxi to Taipei Chiang Kai-Shek International
"Your eyes are so ____."
I thank her.

Li Yu, *To the tune of* The Wave Purifying the Sand

Herbert Giles, footnote to a Pu Song-Ling story entitled _____

Song Emperor Yi-tsu

Herbert Giles, footnote to a Pu Song-Ling story entitled _____

Wikipedia entry on Kaohsiung Incident

Li Yu, *To the tune of* The Wave Purifying the Sand

Li Yu, *To the tune of* Looking South to the River

Daniel Bryant, *Lyric Poets of the Southern T'ang*

Li Yu, *To the tune of* Crow Night Sung

Li Yu, *To the tune of* Crow Night Sung

Herbert Giles, footnote to a Pu Song-Ling story entitled _____

Li Yu, *To the tune of* Beautiful Lady Yu

Ts'ai T'ao commenting on Li Yu's handwriting in *Hsi-ch'ing shih-hua*

All I want is to tell you stories about my life.

For each new friend we make, the past becomes an unintended
  secret.
An invisible hallway unfolds behind each friend's body, hidden from
  view by that friend's newness.
It makes me lonely.

2006

My mother and I are sitting in a café in Cupertino, eating *bao bing*.
—He said you never argued with him about it.
—That's true. Those seemed like the only two options. Afterwards, I
should have just asked for her back, but I found a third option and
decided to pursue that. I'm not going to tell you what that was.
    A rebuke.
    We are tenants in our own context. We keep talking about the time
after her marriage and she presses her hand against her chest.
—It still hurts.

Plane back from the airport
The empire lost
I have seen the remains of his manuscript
Splotched and indistinct for by then
And I would rather not look back at the moonlight
Melanie and the third boy
Yi-Ma very tender at the gate